Saying and Writing Numbers

1 to 10

Name

Date

To parents
Write your child's name and the date in the boxes above. Starting with this page, your child will practice reciting and writing numbers. Acquiring these skills will facilitate an understanding of addition. When your child completes each exercise, please offer lots of praise.

■ Draw a line from 1 to 10 in order while saying each number.

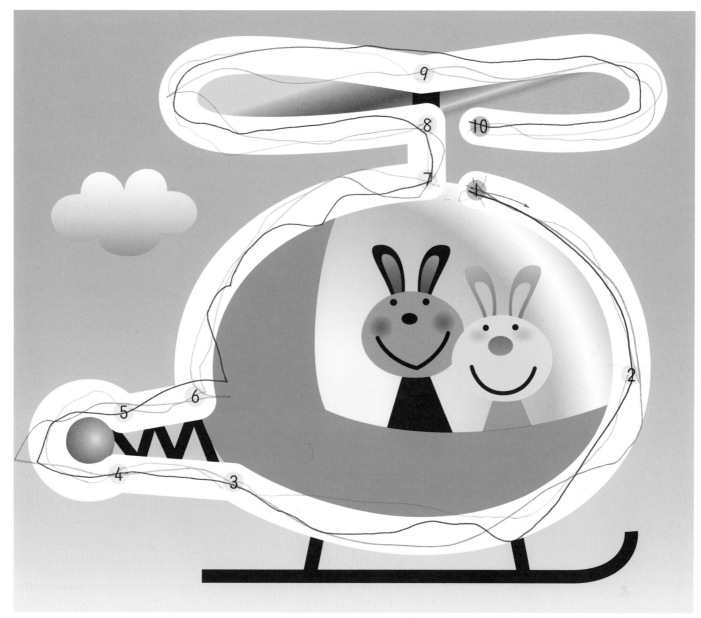

■ Say each number aloud as you trace it.

Ⅰ to ⅠⅠ

■ Draw a line from Ⅰ to ⅠⅠ in order while saying each number.

■ Say each number aloud as you trace it.

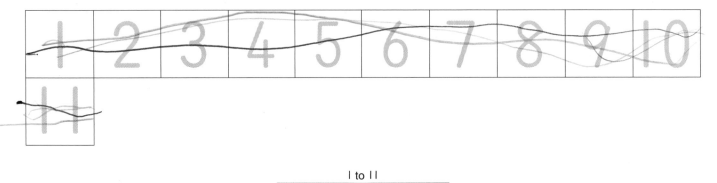

Name

Date

■ Draw a line from 1 to 12 in order while saying each number.

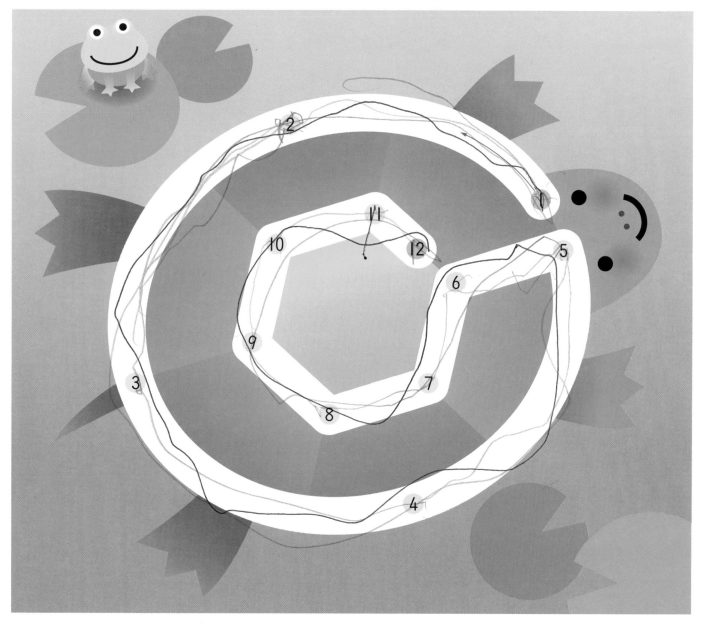

■ Say each number aloud as you trace it.

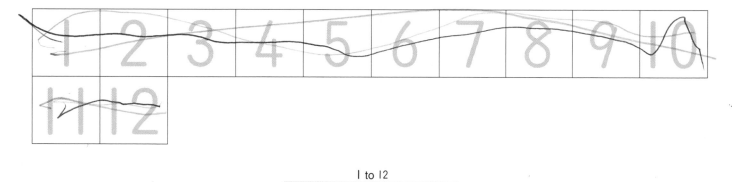

1 to 13

■ Draw a line from 1 to 13 in order while saying each number.

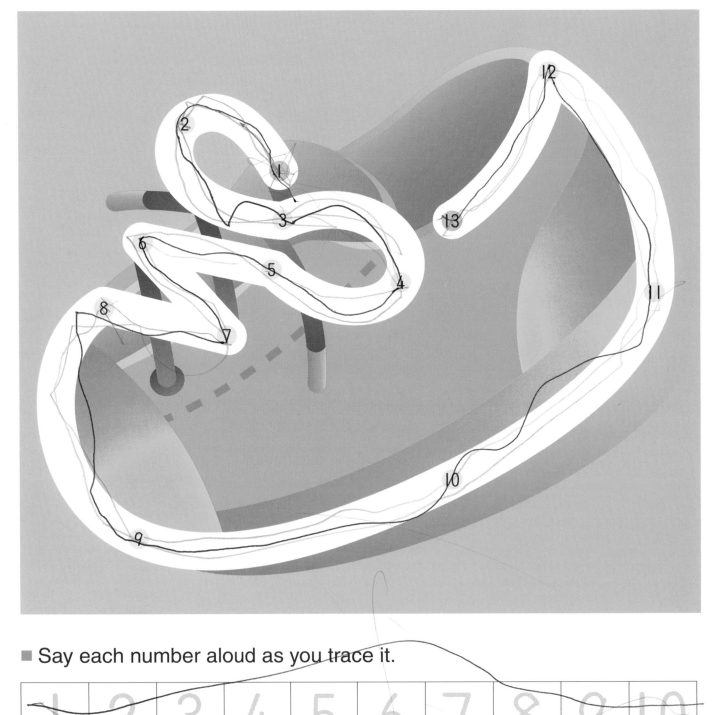

■ Say each number aloud as you trace it.

1	2	3	4	5	6	7	8	9	10
11	12	13							

Name
Date

■ Draw a line from 1 to 14 in order while saying each number.

■ Say each number aloud as you trace it.

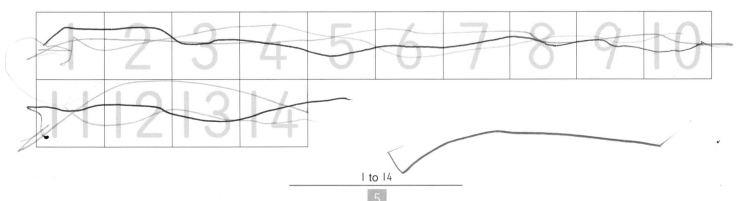

1 to 15

■ Draw a line from 1 to 15 in order while saying each number.

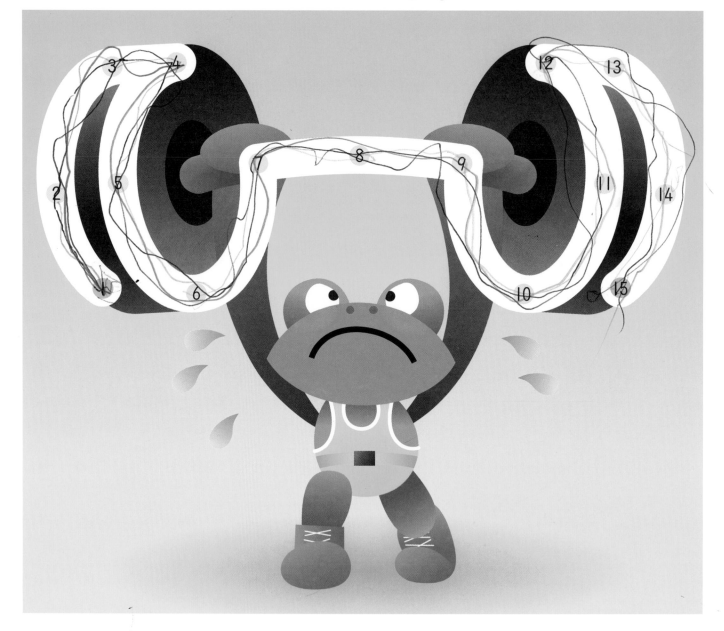

■ Say each number aloud as you trace it.

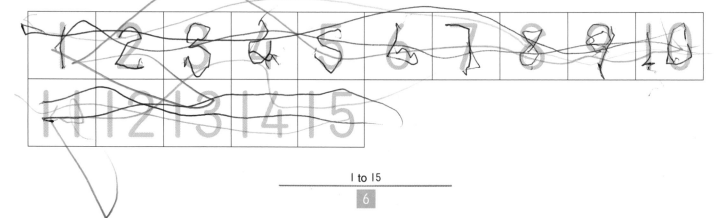

1 to 15

6

Saying and Writing Numbers
1 to 16

Name

Date

■ Draw a line from 1 to 16 in order while saying each number.

■ Say each number aloud as you trace it.

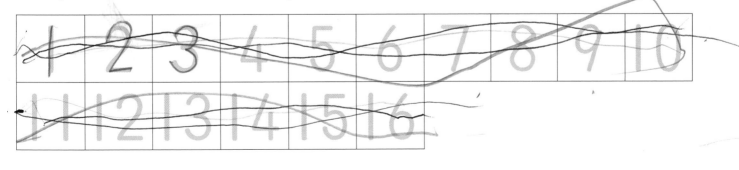

1 to 17

■ Draw a line from 1 to 17 in order while saying each number.

■ Say each number aloud as you trace it.

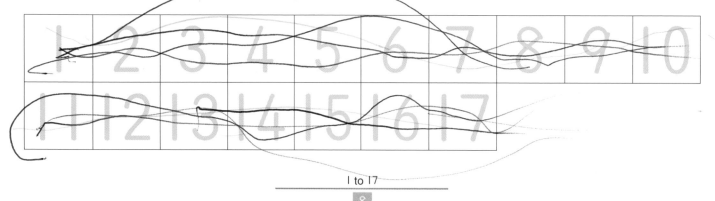

Name
Date

■ Draw a line from 1 to 18 in order while saying each number.

■ Say each number aloud as you trace it.

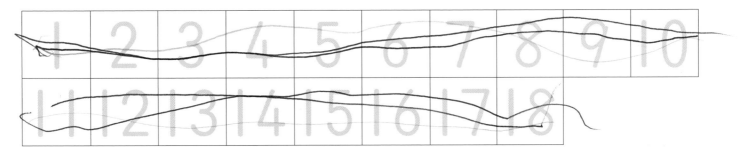

■ Draw a line from 1 to 19 in order while saying each number.

■ Say each number aloud as you trace it.

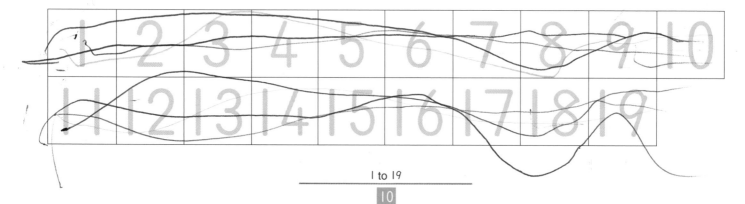

6 Saying and Writing Numbers
1 to 20

Name	
Date	

■ Draw a line from 1 to 20 in order while saying each number.

■ Say each number aloud as you trace it.

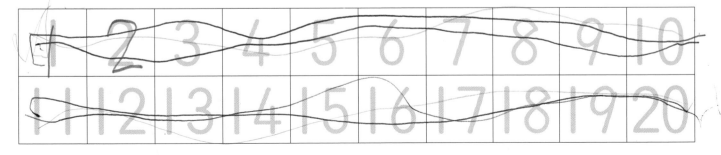

1 to 22

■ Draw a line from 1 to 22 in order while saying each number.

■ Say each number aloud as you trace it.

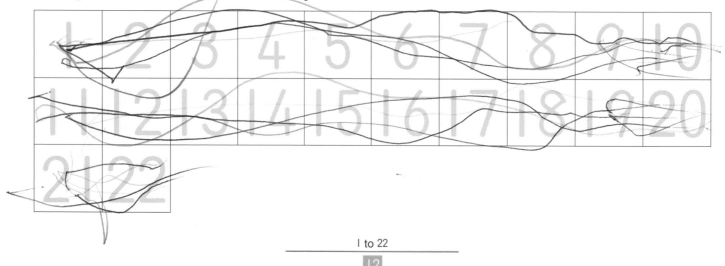

7 Saying and Writing Numbers
1 to 24

Name	
Date	

■ Draw a line from 1 to 24 in order while saying each number.

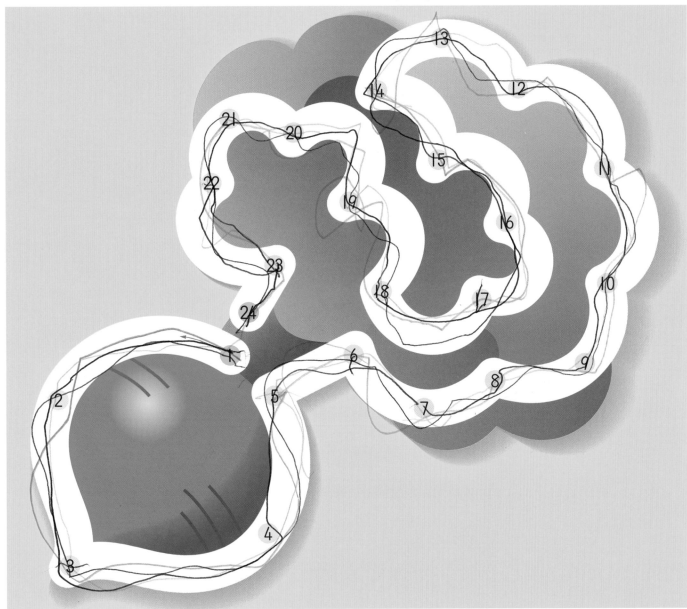

■ Say each number aloud as you trace it.

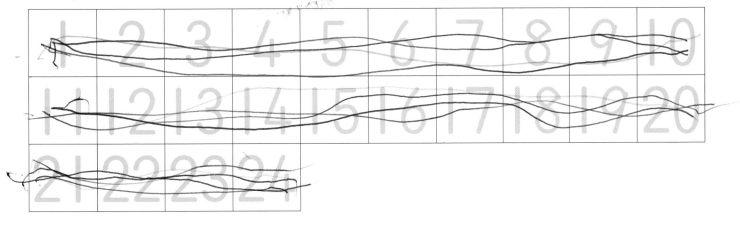

1 to 26

■ Draw a line from 1 to 26 in order while saying each number.

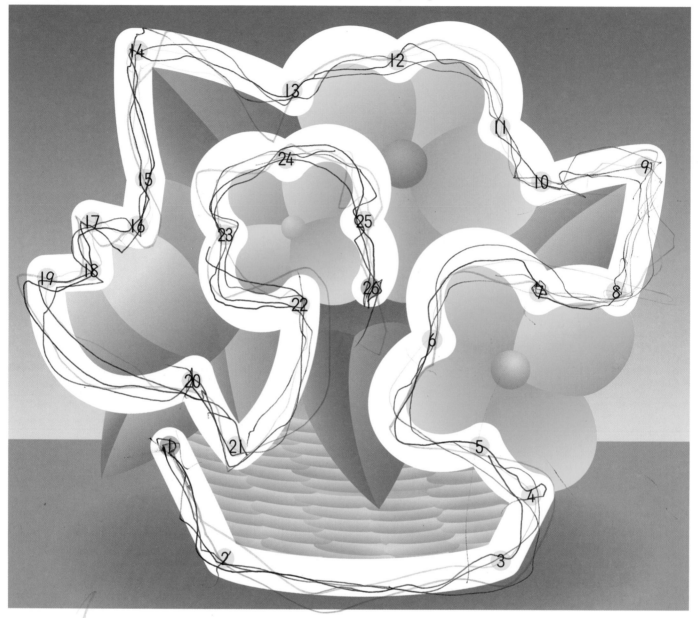

■ Say each number aloud as you trace it.

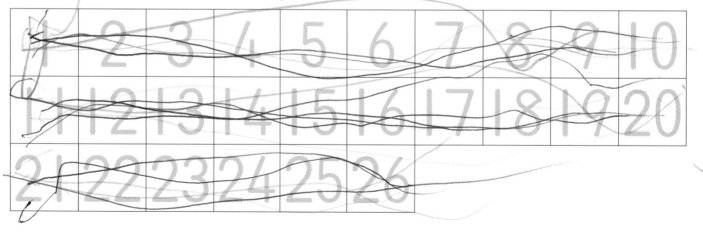

Saying and Writing Numbers
1 to 28

Name

Date

■ Draw a line from 1 to 28 in order while saying each number.

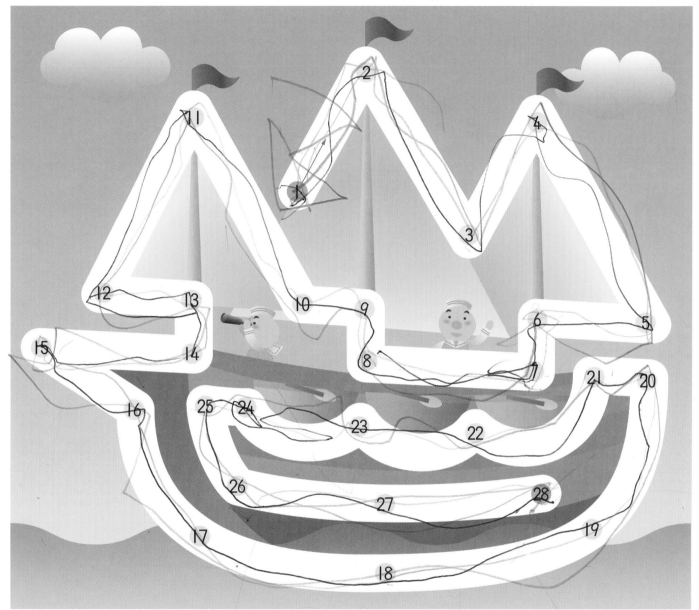

■ Say each number aloud as you trace it.

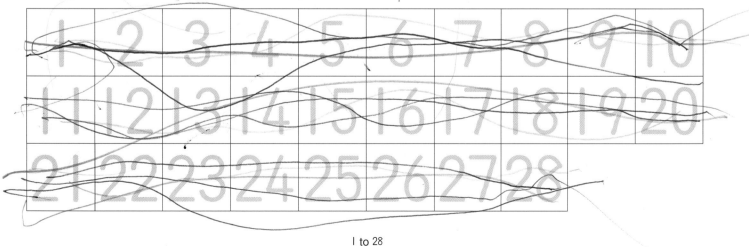

1 to 30

■ Draw a line from 1 to 30 in order while saying each number.

■ Say each number aloud as you trace it.

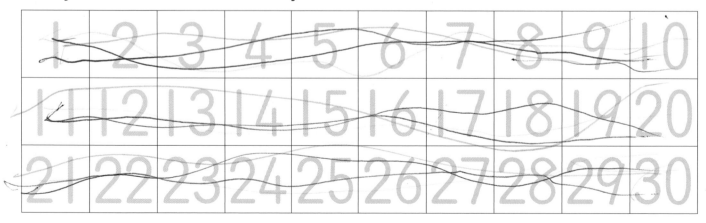

Name

Date

To parents
While your child is writing numbers, please tell him or her that when you add 1 to a number, the result will be the next number.

■ Fill in the missing numbers. Say each number aloud.

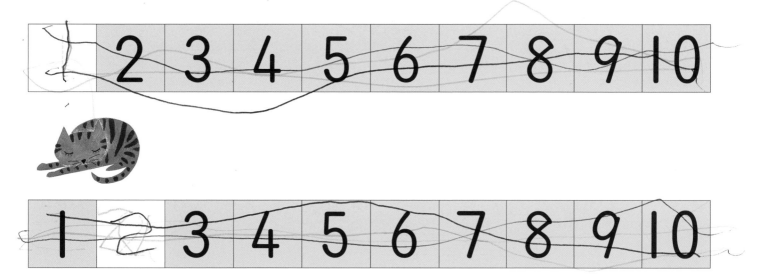

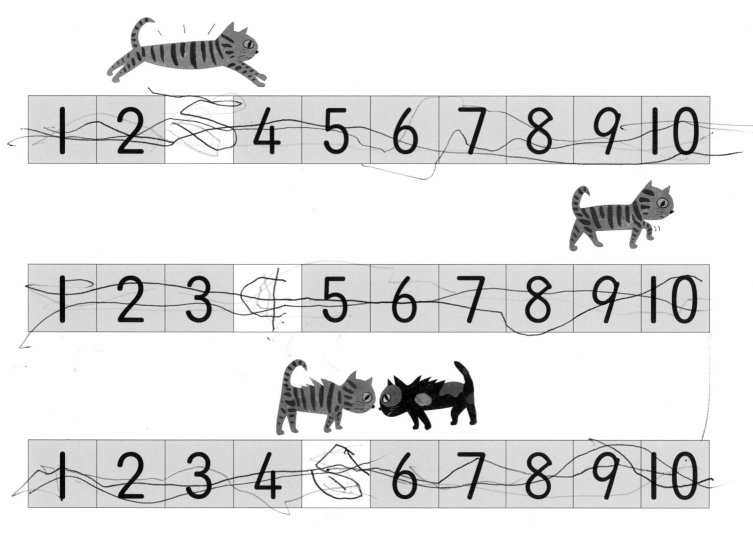

■ Fill in the missing numbers. Say each number aloud.

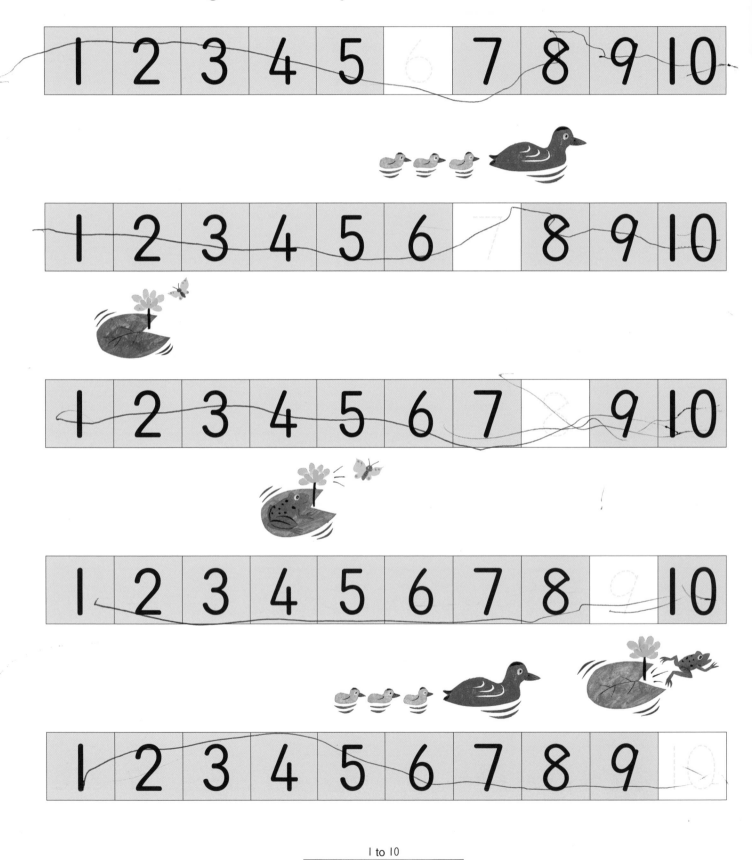

1 2 3 4 5 6 7 8 9 10

1 2 3 4 5 6 7 8 9 10

1 2 3 4 5 6 7 8 9 10

1 2 3 4 5 6 7 8 9 10

1 2 3 4 5 6 7 8 9 10

Saying and Writing Numbers

11 to 20

■ Fill in the missing numbers. Say each number aloud.

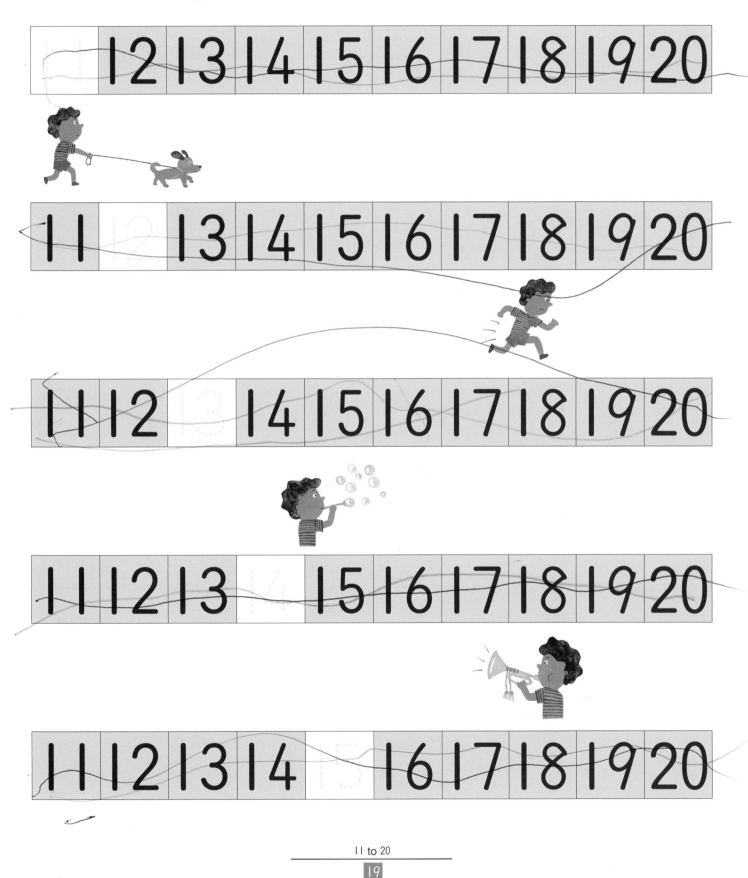

| | 12 | 13 | 14 | 15 | 16 | 17 | 18 | 19 | 20 |

| 11 | | 13 | 14 | 15 | 16 | 17 | 18 | 19 | 20 |

| 11 | 12 | | 14 | 15 | 16 | 17 | 18 | 19 | 20 |

| 11 | 12 | 13 | | 15 | 16 | 17 | 18 | 19 | 20 |

| 11 | 12 | 13 | 14 | | 16 | 17 | 18 | 19 | 20 |

■ Fill in the missing numbers. Say each number aloud.

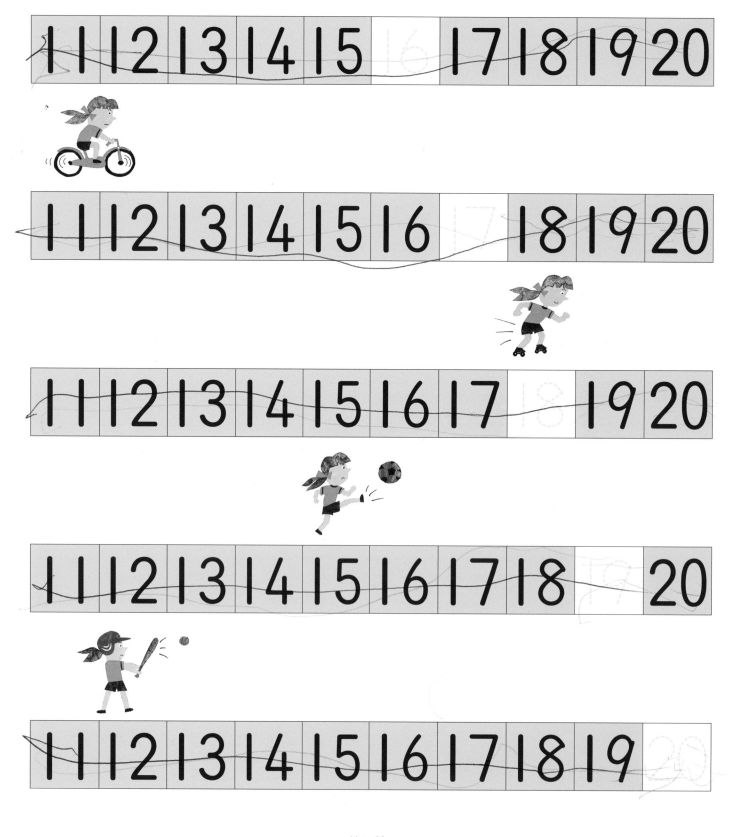

11 12 13 14 15 16 17 18 19 20

11 12 13 14 15 16 17 18 19 20

11 12 13 14 15 16 17 18 19 20

11 12 13 14 15 16 17 18 19 20

11 12 13 14 15 16 17 18 19 20

11 Saying and Writing Numbers
21 to 30

Name

Date

■ Fill in the missing numbers. Say each number aloud.

| 21 | 22 | 23 | 24 | 25 | 26 | 27 | 28 | 29 | 30 |

| 21 | 22 | 23 | 24 | 25 | 26 | 27 | 28 | 29 | 30 |

| 21 | 22 | 23 | 24 | 25 | 26 | 27 | 28 | 29 | 30 |

| 21 | 22 | 23 | 24 | 25 | 26 | 27 | 28 | 29 | 30 |

| 21 | 22 | 23 | 24 | 25 | 26 | 27 | 28 | 29 | 30 |

■ Fill in the missing numbers. Say each number aloud.

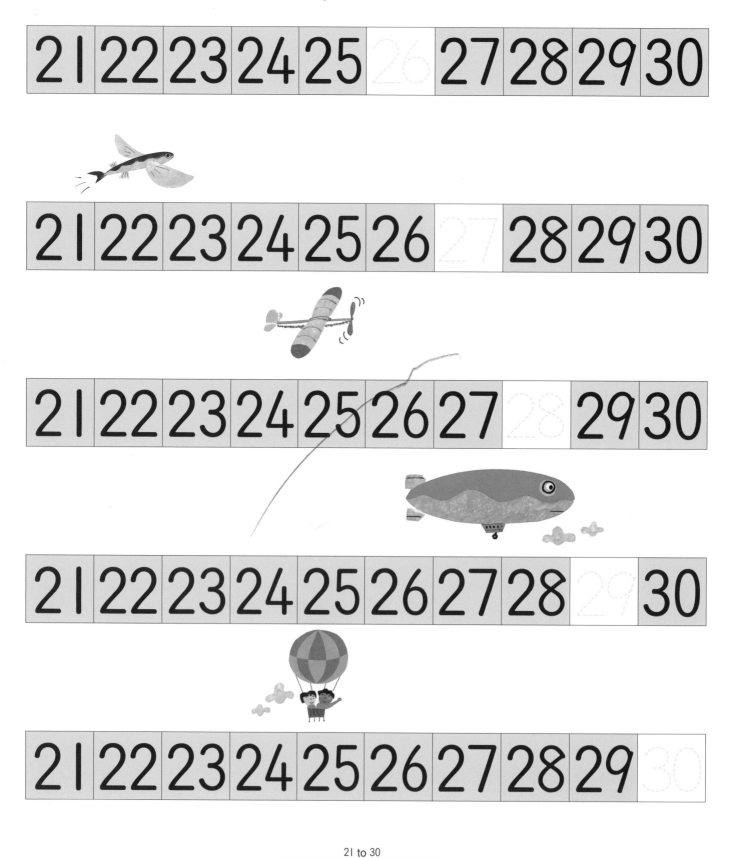

| 21 | 22 | 23 | 24 | 25 | 26 | 27 | 28 | 29 | 30 |

| 21 | 22 | 23 | 24 | 25 | 26 | 27 | 28 | 29 | 30 |

| 21 | 22 | 23 | 24 | 25 | 26 | 27 | 28 | 29 | 30 |

| 21 | 22 | 23 | 24 | 25 | 26 | 27 | 28 | 29 | 30 |

| 21 | 22 | 23 | 24 | 25 | 26 | 27 | 28 | 29 | 30 |

12 Adding 1

1+1 to 9+1

Name

Date

To parents
Please use the number chart to show your child that when you add 1 to a number, the result will be the next number.

■ Fill in the missing numbers and then add the numbers below.

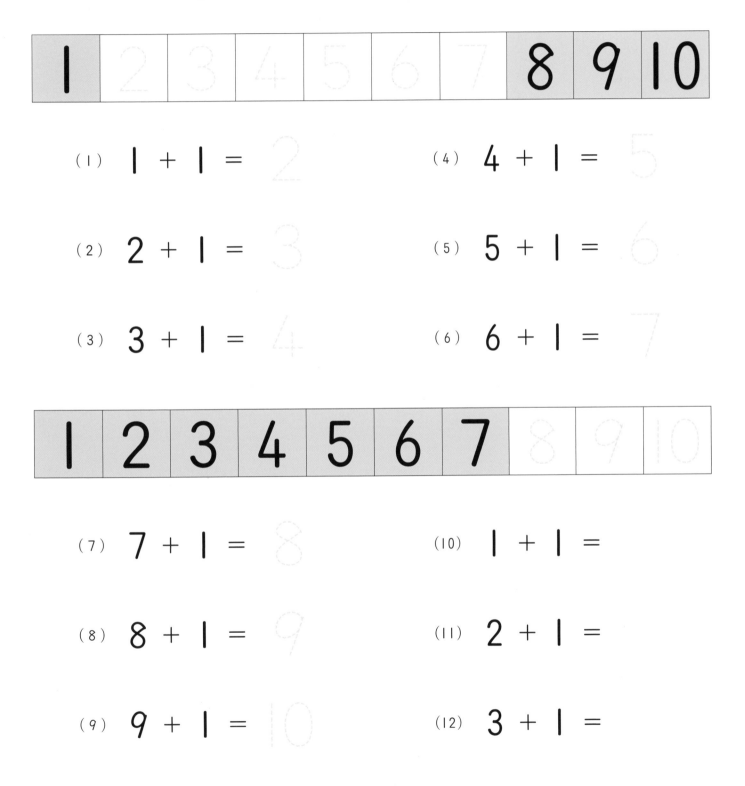

1 2 3 4 5 6 7 8 9 10

(1) 1 + 1 = 2

(2) 2 + 1 = 3

(3) 3 + 1 = 4

(4) 4 + 1 = 5

(5) 5 + 1 = 6

(6) 6 + 1 = 7

1 2 3 4 5 6 7 8 9 10

(7) 7 + 1 = 8

(8) 8 + 1 = 9

(9) 9 + 1 = 10

(10) 1 + 1 =

(11) 2 + 1 =

(12) 3 + 1 =

4+1 to 10+1

■ Fill in the missing numbers and then add the numbers below.

1		3		5		7		9	

(1) 4 + 1 = 5

(2) 5 + 1 = 6

(3) 6 + 1 = 7

(4) 7 + 1 = 8

(5) 8 + 1 =

(6) 9 + 1 =

	2		4		6		8		10
	12	13	14	15	16	17	18	19	20

(7) 10 + 1 =

(8) 8 + 1 =

(9) 7 + 1 =

(10) 9 + 1 =

(11) 6 + 1 =

(12) 10 + 1 =

Name	
Date	

■ Fill in the missing numbers and then add the numbers below.

11	12	13	14	15	16	17	18	19	20

(1) 11 + 1 = 12

(2) 12 + 1 = 13

(3) 13 + 1 = 14

(4) 14 + 1 = 15

(5) 15 + 1 = 16

(6) 16 + 1 = 17

11	12	13	14	15	16	17	18	19	20

(7) 17 + 1 = 18

(8) 18 + 1 = 19

(9) 19 + 1 = 20

(10) 11 + 1 =

(11) 12 + 1 =

(12) 13 + 1 =

14+1 to 20+1

■ Fill in the missing numbers and then add the numbers below.

| 11 | | 13 | | 15 | | 17 | | 19 | |

(1) 14 + 1 = 15

(2) 15 + 1 =

(3) 16 + 1 =

(4) 17 + 1 =

(5) 18 + 1 =

(6) 19 + 1 =

| | 12 | | 14 | | 16 | | 18 | | 20 |
| 21 | 22 | 23 | 24 | 25 | 26 | 27 | 28 | 29 | 30 |

(7) 20 + 1 = 21

(8) 17 + 1 =

(9) 16 + 1 =

(10) 19 + 1 =

(11) 18 + 1 =

(12) 20 + 1 =

Adding 1
21+1 to 29+1

Name	
Date	

■ Fill in the missing numbers and then add the numbers below.

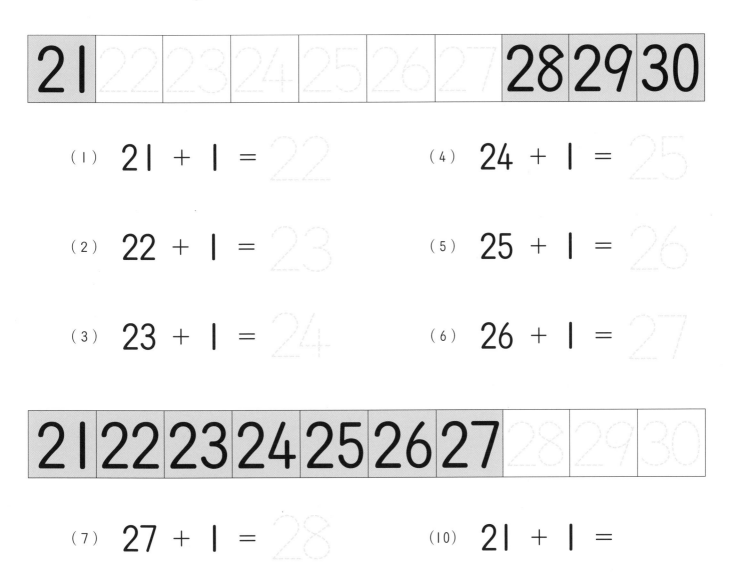

21	22	23	24	25	26	27	28	29	30

(1) 21 + 1 = 22

(2) 22 + 1 = 23

(3) 23 + 1 = 24

(4) 24 + 1 = 25

(5) 25 + 1 = 26

(6) 26 + 1 = 27

21	22	23	24	25	26	27	28	29	30

(7) 27 + 1 = 28

(8) 28 + 1 = 29

(9) 29 + 1 = 30

(10) 21 + 1 =

(11) 22 + 1 =

(12) 23 + 1 =

■ Fill in the missing numbers and then add the numbers below.

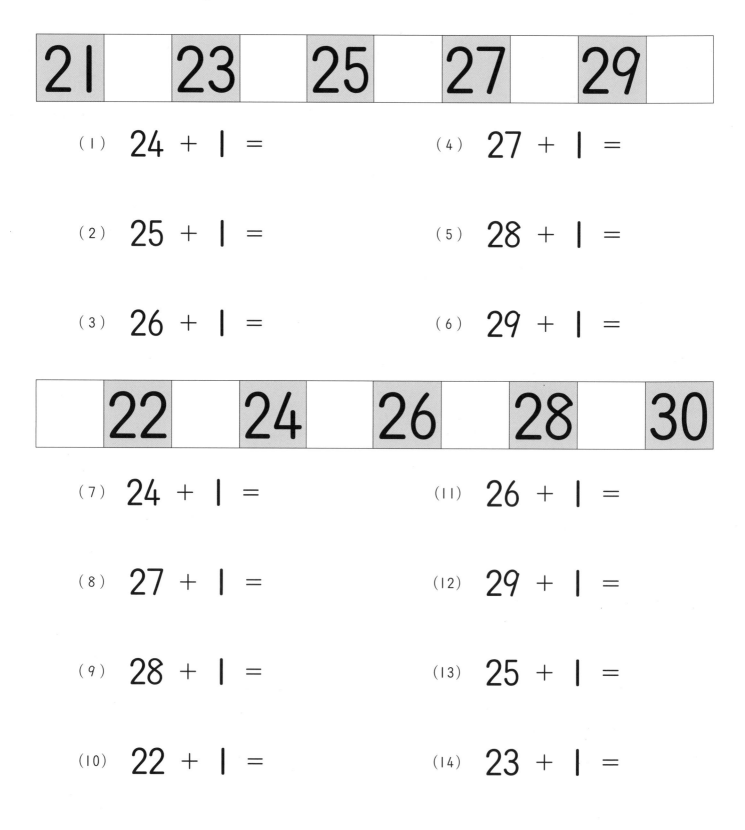

| 21 | | 23 | | 25 | | 27 | | 29 | |

(1) 24 + 1 =

(2) 25 + 1 =

(3) 26 + 1 =

(4) 27 + 1 =

(5) 28 + 1 =

(6) 29 + 1 =

| | 22 | | 24 | | 26 | | 28 | | 30 |

(7) 24 + 1 =

(8) 27 + 1 =

(9) 28 + 1 =

(10) 22 + 1 =

(11) 26 + 1 =

(12) 29 + 1 =

(13) 25 + 1 =

(14) 23 + 1 =

15 Adding 1

1+1 to 27+1

■ Fill in the missing numbers and then add the numbers below.

1		3		5		7		9	
	12		14		16		18		20
21		23		25		27		29	30

(1) 1 + 1 =

(2) 3 + 1 =

(3) 5 + 1 =

(4) 7 + 1 =

(5) 9 + 1 =

(6) 10 + 1 =

(7) 12 + 1 =

(8) 14 + 1 =

(9) 16 + 1 =

(10) 18 + 1 =

(11) 21 + 1 =

(12) 23 + 1 =

(13) 25 + 1 =

(14) 27 + 1 =

2+1 to 29+1

■ Fill in the missing numbers and then add the numbers below.

1	2		4		6		8		10
11		13		15		17		19	
	22		24		26		28		

(1) 2 + 1 =

(2) 4 + 1 =

(3) 6 + 1 =

(4) 8 + 1 =

(5) 11 + 1 =

(6) 13 + 1 =

(7) 15 + 1 =

(8) 17 + 1 =

(9) 19 + 1 =

(10) 20 + 1 =

(11) 22 + 1 =

(12) 24 + 1 =

(13) 26 + 1 =

(14) 28 + 1 =

(15) 29 + 1 =

Adding 1

1+1 to 4+1

Name
Date

To parents
Learning to add 1 is a basic step towards successfully understanding addition. Starting with this page, your child will repeatedly practice formulas that include the number 1 in order to gain solid calculation abilities. Some pages contain a number chart to give children a hint that the answers are included in the chart.

■ Add the numbers below.

(1) $1 + 1 =$

(2) $2 + 1 =$

(3) $3 + 1 =$

(4) $4 + 1 =$

(5) $1 + 1 =$

(6) $3 + 1 =$

(7) $2 + 1 =$

(8) $4 + 1 =$

(9) $2 + 1 =$

(10) $4 + 1 =$

(11) $1 + 1 =$

(12) $3 + 1 =$

(13) $4 + 1 =$

(14) $3 + 1 =$

(15) $1 + 1 =$

(16) $2 + 1 =$

(17) $3 + 1 =$

(18) $4 + 1 =$

(19) $2 + 1 =$

(20) $1 + 1 =$

1	2	3	4	5

5+1 to 9+1

■ Add the numbers below.

(1) $5 + 1 =$

(2) $6 + 1 =$

(3) $7 + 1 =$

(4) $8 + 1 =$

(5) $9 + 1 =$

(6) $5 + 1 =$

(7) $7 + 1 =$

(8) $6 + 1 =$

(9) $9 + 1 =$

(10) $8 + 1 =$

(11) $6 + 1 =$

(12) $7 + 1 =$

(13) $5 + 1 =$

(14) $8 + 1 =$

(15) $9 + 1 =$

(16) $7 + 1 =$

(17) $5 + 1 =$

(18) $8 + 1 =$

(19) $6 + 1 =$

(20) $9 + 1 =$

1	2	3	4	5	6	7	8	9	10

Adding 1

1+1 to 9+1

■ Add the numbers below.

(1) 1 + 1 =

(2) 3 + 1 =

(3) 4 + 1 =

(4) 2 + 1 =

(5) 7 + 1 =

(6) 5 + 1 =

(7) 6 + 1 =

(8) 9 + 1 =

(9) 8 + 1 =

(10) 6 + 1 =

(11) 9 + 1 =

(12) 3 + 1 =

(13) 4 + 1 =

(14) 7 + 1 =

(15) 2 + 1 =

(16) 5 + 1 =

(17) 8 + 1 =

(18) 1 + 1 =

(19) 5 + 1 =

(20) 9 + 1 =

1	2	3	4	5	6	7	8	9	10

■ Add the numbers below.

(1) 2 + 1 =

(2) 5 + 1 =

(3) 6 + 1 =

(4) 8 + 1 =

(5) 9 + 1 =

(6) 7 + 1 =

(7) 4 + 1 =

(8) 1 + 1 =

(9) 3 + 1 =

(10) 1 + 1 =

(11) 8 + 1 =

(12) 9 + 1 =

(13) 4 + 1 =

(14) 6 + 1 =

(15) 7 + 1 =

(16) 5 + 1 =

(17) 2 + 1 =

(18) 3 + 1 =

(19) 2 + 1 =

(20) 8 + 1 =

| 1 | 2 | 3 | 4 | 5 | 6 | 7 | 8 | 9 | 10 |

Adding 1

10+1 to 14+1

Name	
Date	

■ Add the numbers below.

(1) $10 + 1 =$

(2) $11 + 1 =$

(3) $12 + 1 =$

(4) $13 + 1 =$

(5) $14 + 1 =$

(6) $11 + 1 =$

(7) $12 + 1 =$

(8) $10 + 1 =$

(9) $14 + 1 =$

(10) $13 + 1 =$

(11) $11 + 1 =$

(12) $10 + 1 =$

(13) $14 + 1 =$

(14) $13 + 1 =$

(15) $12 + 1 =$

(16) $10 + 1 =$

(17) $13 + 1 =$

(18) $14 + 1 =$

(19) $12 + 1 =$

(20) $11 + 1 =$

| 11 | 12 | 13 | 14 | 15 |

15+1 to 19+1

■ Add the numbers below.

(1) 15 + 1 =

(2) 16 + 1 =

(3) 17 + 1 =

(4) 18 + 1 =

(5) 19 + 1 =

(6) 15 + 1 =

(7) 17 + 1 =

(8) 16 + 1 =

(9) 19 + 1 =

(10) 18 + 1 =

(11) 16 + 1 =

(12) 17 + 1 =

(13) 15 + 1 =

(14) 18 + 1 =

(15) 19 + 1 =

(16) 17 + 1 =

(17) 15 + 1 =

(18) 18 + 1 =

(19) 16 + 1 =

(20) 19 + 1 =

| 11 | 12 | 13 | 14 | 15 | 16 | 17 | 18 | 19 | 20 |

Name

Date

■ Add the numbers below.

(1) $10 + 1 =$

(2) $11 + 1 =$

(3) $12 + 1 =$

(4) $14 + 1 =$

(5) $13 + 1 =$

(6) $16 + 1 =$

(7) $17 + 1 =$

(8) $15 + 1 =$

(9) $19 + 1 =$

(10) $18 + 1 =$

(11) $15 + 1 =$

(12) $17 + 1 =$

(13) $19 + 1 =$

(14) $11 + 1 =$

(15) $13 + 1 =$

(16) $12 + 1 =$

(17) $14 + 1 =$

(18) $16 + 1 =$

(19) $18 + 1 =$

(20) $10 + 1 =$

| 11 | 12 | 13 | 14 | 15 | 16 | 17 | 18 | 19 | 20 |

■ Add the numbers below.

(1) 12 + 1 =

(2) 15 + 1 =

(3) 16 + 1 =

(4) 18 + 1 =

(5) 19 + 1 =

(6) 17 + 1 =

(7) 14 + 1 =

(8) 11 + 1 =

(9) 13 + 1 =

(10) 10 + 1 =

(11) 18 + 1 =

(12) 19 + 1 =

(13) 10 + 1 =

(14) 16 + 1 =

(15) 17 + 1 =

(16) 15 + 1 =

(17) 12 + 1 =

(18) 13 + 1 =

(19) 14 + 1 =

(20) 11 + 1 =

| 11 | 12 | 13 | 14 | 15 | 16 | 17 | 18 | 19 | 20 |

Name

Date

■ Add the numbers below.

(1) $13 + 1 =$

(2) $15 + 1 =$

(3) $11 + 1 =$

(4) $14 + 1 =$

(5) $17 + 1 =$

(6) $8 + 1 =$

(7) $5 + 1 =$

(8) $4 + 1 =$

(9) $1 + 1 =$

(10) $6 + 1 =$

(11) $2 + 1 =$

(12) $18 + 1 =$

(13) $7 + 1 =$

(14) $19 + 1 =$

(15) $3 + 1 =$

(16) $10 + 1 =$

(17) $9 + 1 =$

(18) $12 + 1 =$

(19) $16 + 1 =$

(20) $5 + 1 =$

1	2	3	4	5	6	7	8	9	10	11	12	13	14	15	16	17	18	19	20

■ Add the numbers below.

(1) $19 + 1 =$

(2) $15 + 1 =$

(3) $2 + 1 =$

(4) $4 + 1 =$

(5) $8 + 1 =$

(6) $6 + 1 =$

(7) $3 + 1 =$

(8) $1 + 1 =$

(9) $14 + 1 =$

(10) $10 + 1 =$

(11) $5 + 1 =$

(12) $13 + 1 =$

(13) $16 + 1 =$

(14) $7 + 1 =$

(15) $11 + 1 =$

(16) $9 + 1 =$

(17) $12 + 1 =$

(18) $18 + 1 =$

(19) $17 + 1 =$

(20) $6 + 1 =$

| 1 | 2 | 3 | 4 | 5 | 6 | 7 | 8 | 9 | 10 | 11 | 12 | 13 | 14 | 15 | 16 | 17 | 18 | 19 | 20 |

Adding 1

20+1 to 24+1

■ Add the numbers below.

(1) 20 + 1 =

(2) 21 + 1 =

(3) 22 + 1 =

(4) 23 + 1 =

(5) 24 + 1 =

(6) 21 + 1 =

(7) 22 + 1 =

(8) 20 + 1 =

(9) 24 + 1 =

(10) 23 + 1 =

(11) 21 + 1 =

(12) 20 + 1 =

(13) 24 + 1 =

(14) 23 + 1 =

(15) 22 + 1 =

(16) 21 + 1 =

(17) 23 + 1 =

(18) 24 + 1 =

(19) 20 + 1 =

(20) 22 + 1 =

21 22 23 24 25

25 + 1 to 29 + 1

■ Add the numbers below.

(1) 25 + 1 =

(2) 26 + 1 =

(3) 27 + 1 =

(4) 28 + 1 =

(5) 29 + 1 =

(6) 25 + 1 =

(7) 27 + 1 =

(8) 26 + 1 =

(9) 29 + 1 =

(10) 28 + 1 =

(11) 28 + 1 =

(12) 27 + 1 =

(13) 25 + 1 =

(14) 26 + 1 =

(15) 29 + 1 =

(16) 27 + 1 =

(17) 25 + 1 =

(18) 28 + 1 =

(19) 26 + 1 =

(20) 29 + 1 =

| 21 | 22 | 23 | 24 | 25 | 26 | 27 | 28 | 29 | 30 |

22 Adding 1
20 + 1 to 29 + 1

Name

Date

■ Add the numbers below.

(1) 22 + 1 =

(2) 20 + 1 =

(3) 21 + 1 =

(4) 24 + 1 =

(5) 25 + 1 =

(6) 23 + 1 =

(7) 26 + 1 =

(8) 28 + 1 =

(9) 29 + 1 =

(10) 27 + 1 =

(11) 23 + 1 =

(12) 27 + 1 =

(13) 25 + 1 =

(14) 21 + 1 =

(15) 24 + 1 =

(16) 29 + 1 =

(17) 26 + 1 =

(18) 22 + 1 =

(19) 20 + 1 =

(20) 28 + 1 =

| 21 | 22 | 23 | 24 | 25 | 26 | 27 | 28 | 29 | 30 |

■ Add the numbers below.

(1) 27 + 1 =

(2) 24 + 1 =

(3) 29 + 1 =

(4) 22 + 1 =

(5) 20 + 1 =

(6) 23 + 1 =

(7) 21 + 1 =

(8) 25 + 1 =

(9) 26 + 1 =

(10) 28 + 1 =

(11) 24 + 1 =

(12) 20 + 1 =

(13) 29 + 1 =

(14) 21 + 1 =

(15) 28 + 1 =

(16) 22 + 1 =

(17) 25 + 1 =

(18) 27 + 1 =

(19) 23 + 1 =

(20) 26 + 1 =

21 22 23 24 25 26 27 28 29 30

Name

Date

■ Add the numbers below.

(1) $12 + 1 =$

(2) $13 + 1 =$

(3) $11 + 1 =$

(4) $15 + 1 =$

(5) $10 + 1 =$

(6) $16 + 1 =$

(7) $14 + 1 =$

(8) $19 + 1 =$

(9) $17 + 1 =$

(10) $18 + 1 =$

(11) $22 + 1 =$

(12) $23 + 1 =$

(13) $20 + 1 =$

(14) $21 + 1 =$

(15) $25 + 1 =$

(16) $26 + 1 =$

(17) $24 + 1 =$

(18) $28 + 1 =$

(19) $27 + 1 =$

(20) $29 + 1 =$

| 11 | 12 | 13 | 14 | 15 | 16 | 17 | 18 | 19 | 20 | 21 | 22 | 23 | 24 | 25 | 26 | 27 | 28 | 29 | 30 |

■ Add the numbers below.

(1) $19 + 1 =$

(2) $14 + 1 =$

(3) $22 + 1 =$

(4) $29 + 1 =$

(5) $11 + 1 =$

(6) $15 + 1 =$

(7) $20 + 1 =$

(8) $17 + 1 =$

(9) $26 + 1 =$

(10) $24 + 1 =$

(11) $27 + 1 =$

(12) $21 + 1 =$

(13) $10 + 1 =$

(14) $18 + 1 =$

(15) $25 + 1 =$

(16) $13 + 1 =$

(17) $28 + 1 =$

(18) $23 + 1 =$

(19) $12 + 1 =$

(20) $16 + 1 =$

| 11 | 12 | 13 | 14 | 15 | 16 | 17 | 18 | 19 | 20 | 21 | 22 | 23 | 24 | 25 | 26 | 27 | 28 | 29 | 30 |

Saying and Writing Numbers

1 to 10

Name

Date

To parents
While your child is writing numbers, please tell him or her that when you
add 2 to a number, the result will be the number after the next number.

■ Fill in the missing numbers. Say each number aloud.

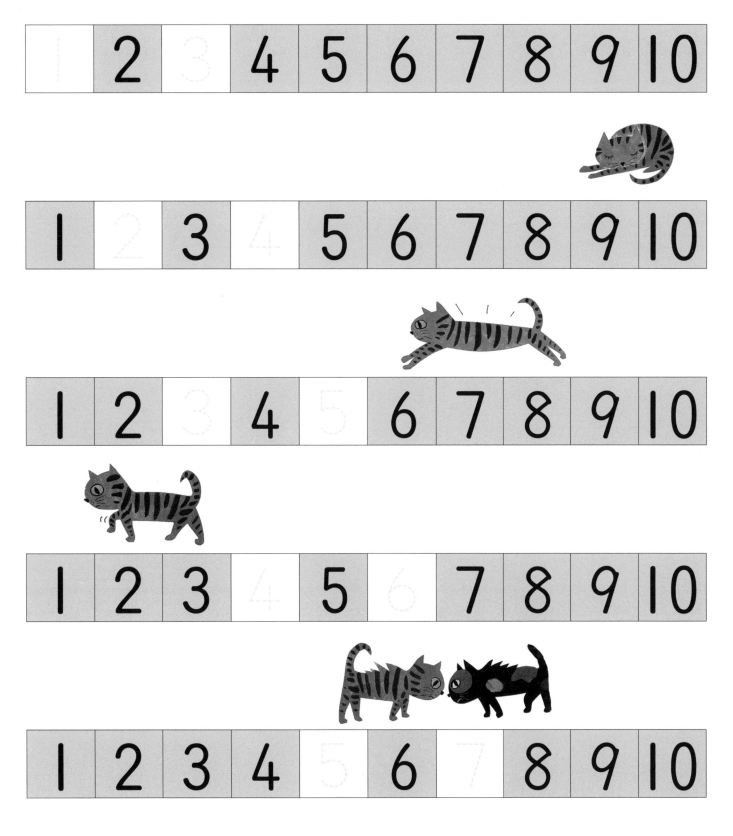

6 to 15

■ Fill in the missing numbers. Say each number aloud.

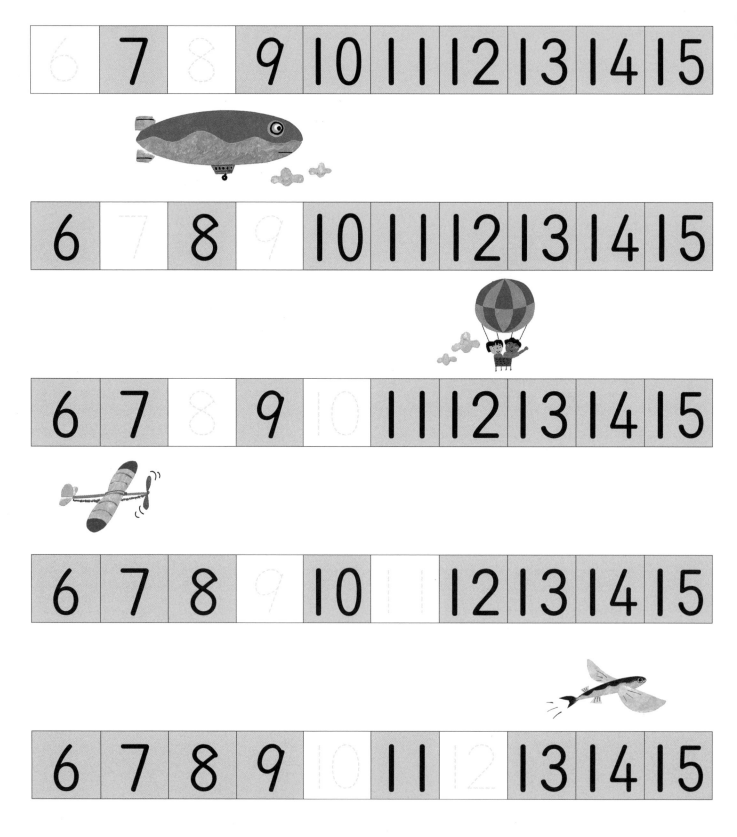

6 | 7 | 8 | 9 | 10 | 11 | 12 | 13 | 14 | 15

6 | 7 | 8 | 9 | 10 | 11 | 12 | 13 | 14 | 15

6 | 7 | 8 | 9 | 10 | 11 | 12 | 13 | 14 | 15

6 | 7 | 8 | 9 | 10 | 11 | 12 | 13 | 14 | 15

6 | 7 | 8 | 9 | 10 | 11 | 12 | 13 | 14 | 15

Saying and Writing Numbers
11 to 20

Name

Date

■ Fill in the missing numbers. Say each number aloud.

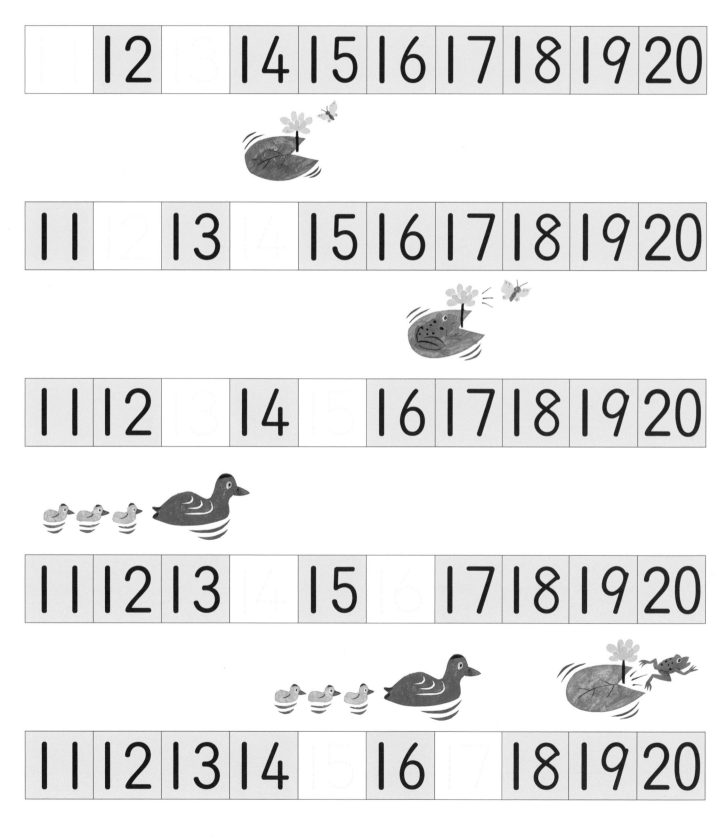

| | 12 | | 14 | 15 | 16 | 17 | 18 | 19 | 20 |

| 11 | | 13 | | 15 | 16 | 17 | 18 | 19 | 20 |

| 11 | 12 | | 14 | | 16 | 17 | 18 | 19 | 20 |

| 11 | 12 | 13 | | 15 | | 17 | 18 | 19 | 20 |

| 11 | 12 | 13 | 14 | | 16 | | 18 | 19 | 20 |

16 to 25

Fill in the missing numbers. Say each number aloud.

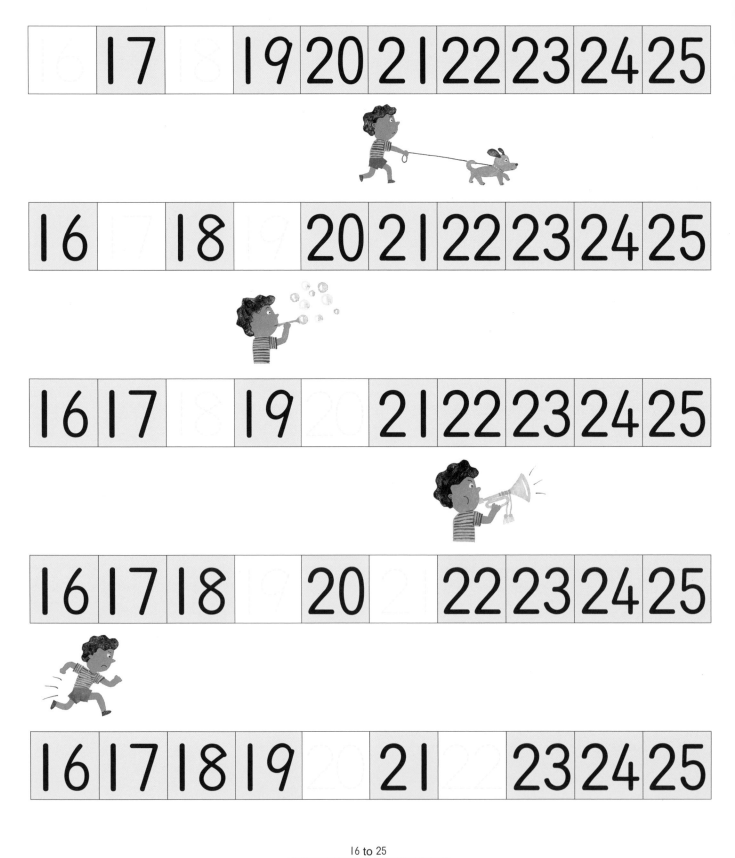

| | 17 | | 19 | 20 | 21 | 22 | 23 | 24 | 25 |

| 16 | | 18 | | 20 | 21 | 22 | 23 | 24 | 25 |

| 16 | 17 | | 19 | | 21 | 22 | 23 | 24 | 25 |

| 16 | 17 | 18 | | 20 | | 22 | 23 | 24 | 25 |

| 16 | 17 | 18 | 19 | | 21 | | 23 | 24 | 25 |

26 Saying and Writing Numbers
21 to 30

Name

Date

■ Fill in the missing numbers. Say each number aloud.

	22		24	25	26	27	28	29	30

21		23		25	26	27	28	29	30

21	22		24		26	27	28	29	30

21	22	23		25		27	28	29	30

21	22	23	24		26		28	29	30

26 to 35

■ Fill in the missing numbers. Say each number aloud.

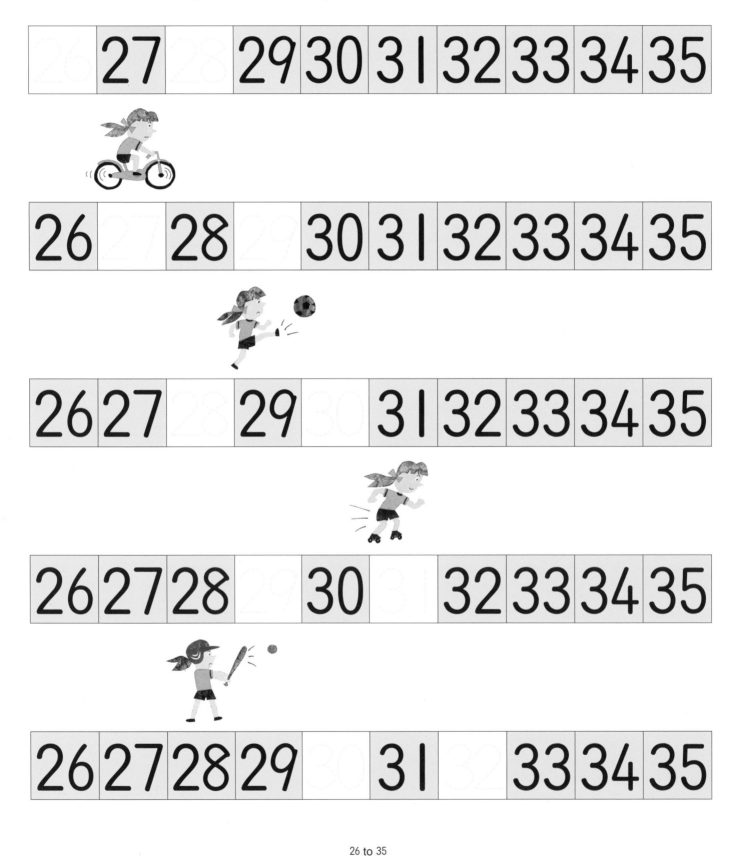

| | 27 | | 29 | 30 | 31 | 32 | 33 | 34 | 35 |

| 26 | | 28 | | 30 | 31 | 32 | 33 | 34 | 35 |

| 26 | 27 | | 29 | | 31 | 32 | 33 | 34 | 35 |

| 26 | 27 | 28 | | 30 | | 32 | 33 | 34 | 35 |

| 26 | 27 | 28 | 29 | | 31 | | 33 | 34 | 35 |

27 Adding 2
1+2 to 9+2

Name

Date

To parents
Please use the number chart to help your child understand that when you add 2 to a number, the result will be the number after the next number.

■ Fill in the missing numbers and then add the numbers below.

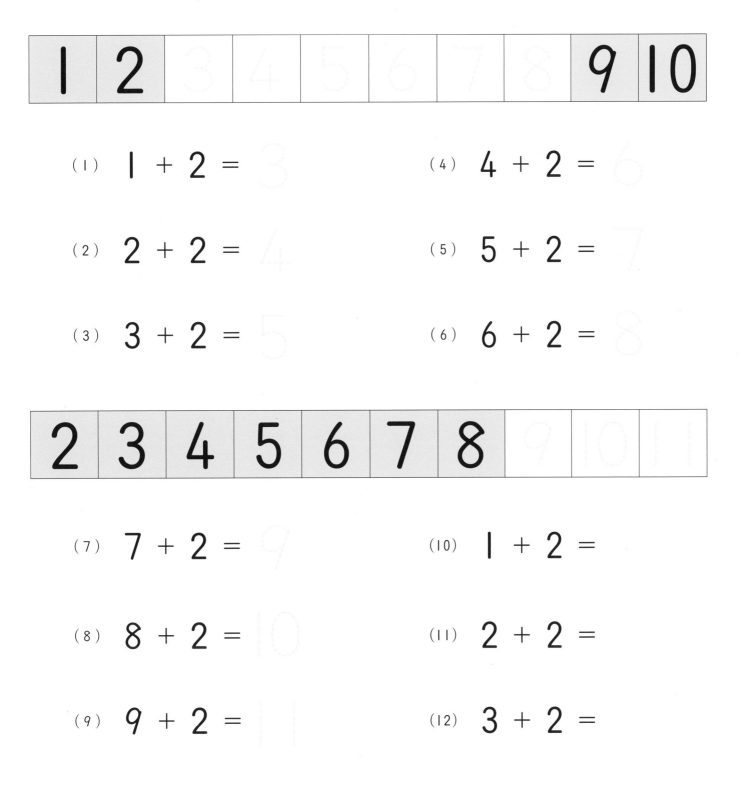

| 1 | 2 | 3 | 4 | 5 | 6 | 7 | 8 | 9 | 10 |

(1) 1 + 2 =

(2) 2 + 2 =

(3) 3 + 2 =

(4) 4 + 2 =

(5) 5 + 2 =

(6) 6 + 2 =

| 2 | 3 | 4 | 5 | 6 | 7 | 8 | 9 | 10 | 11 |

(7) 7 + 2 =

(8) 8 + 2 =

(9) 9 + 2 =

(10) 1 + 2 =

(11) 2 + 2 =

(12) 3 + 2 =

4+2 to 10+2

■ Fill in the missing numbers and then add the numbers below.

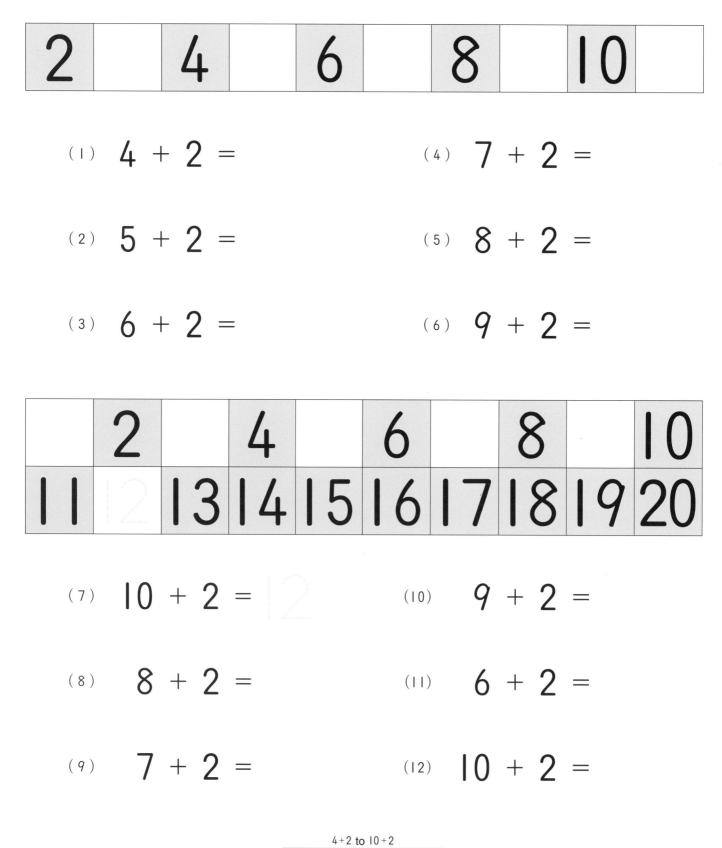

| 2 | | 4 | | 6 | | 8 | | 10 | |

(1) 4 + 2 =

(2) 5 + 2 =

(3) 6 + 2 =

(4) 7 + 2 =

(5) 8 + 2 =

(6) 9 + 2 =

| | 2 | | 4 | | 6 | | 8 | | 10 |
| 11 | 12 | 13 | 14 | 15 | 16 | 17 | 18 | 19 | 20 |

(7) 10 + 2 =

(8) 8 + 2 =

(9) 7 + 2 =

(10) 9 + 2 =

(11) 6 + 2 =

(12) 10 + 2 =

Adding 2

11 + 2 to 19 + 2

Name	
Date	

■ Fill in the missing numbers and then add the numbers below.

11	12	13	14	15	16	17	18	19	20

(1) 11 + 2 =

(2) 12 + 2 =

(3) 13 + 2 =

(4) 14 + 2 =

(5) 15 + 2 =

(6) 16 + 2 =

12	13	14	15	16	17	18	19	20	21

(7) 17 + 2 =

(8) 18 + 2 =

(9) 19 + 2 =

(10) 11 + 2 =

(11) 12 + 2 =

(12) 13 + 2 =

14+2 to 20+2

■ Fill in the missing numbers and then add the numbers below.

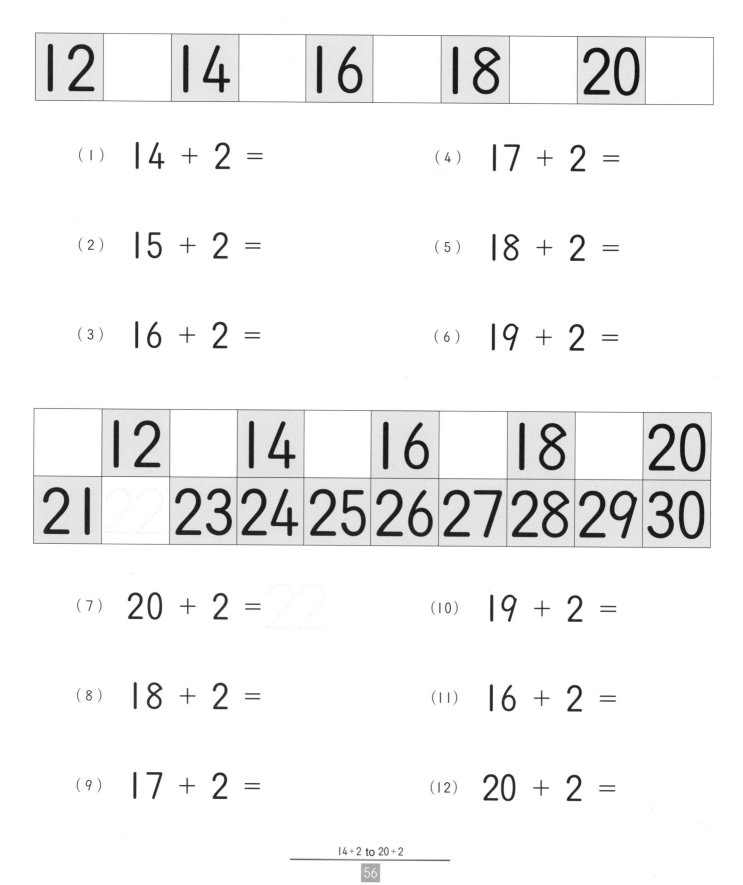

| 12 | | 14 | | 16 | | 18 | | 20 | |

(1) 14 + 2 =

(4) 17 + 2 =

(2) 15 + 2 =

(5) 18 + 2 =

(3) 16 + 2 =

(6) 19 + 2 =

	12		14		16		18		20
21	22	23	24	25	26	27	28	29	30

(7) 20 + 2 = 22

(10) 19 + 2 =

(8) 18 + 2 =

(11) 16 + 2 =

(9) 17 + 2 =

(12) 20 + 2 =

Adding 2
21 + 2 to 28 + 2

Name

Date

■ Fill in the missing numbers and then add the numbers below.

21	22							29	30

(1) 21 + 2 =

(2) 22 + 2 =

(3) 23 + 2 =

(4) 24 + 2 =

(5) 25 + 2 =

(6) 26 + 2 =

21	22	23	24	25	26	27	28		

(7) 27 + 2 =

(8) 28 + 2 =

(9) 21 + 2 =

(10) 22 + 2 =

(11) 23 + 2 =

(12) 24 + 2 =

■ Fill in the missing numbers and then add the numbers below.

| 21 | | 23 | | 25 | | 27 | | 29 | |

(1) 25 + 2 =

(2) 26 + 2 =

(3) 27 + 2 =

(4) 28 + 2 =

(5) 27 + 2 =

(6) 21 + 2 =

| | 22 | | 24 | | 26 | | 28 | | 30 |

(7) 28 + 2 =

(8) 24 + 2 =

(9) 26 + 2 =

(10) 25 + 2 =

(11) 27 + 2 =

(12) 22 + 2 =

(13) 28 + 2 =

(14) 23 + 2 =

Adding 2

1+2 to 27+2

Name
Date

■ Fill in the missing numbers and then add the numbers below.

1	2		4		6		8		10
11		13		15		17		19	
	22		24		26		28		30

(1) 1 + 2 =

(2) 3 + 2 =

(3) 5 + 2 =

(4) 7 + 2 =

(5) 10 + 2 =

(6) 12 + 2 =

(7) 14 + 2 =

(8) 16 + 2 =

(9) 18 + 2 =

(10) 19 + 2 =

(11) 21 + 2 =

(12) 23 + 2 =

(13) 25 + 2 =

(14) 27 + 2 =

2+2 to 28+2

■ Fill in the missing numbers and then add the numbers below.

1	2	3		5		7		9	
	12		14		16		18		20
21		23		25		27		29	

(1) 2 + 2 =

(2) 4 + 2 =

(3) 6 + 2 =

(4) 8 + 2 =

(5) 9 + 2 =

(6) 11 + 2 =

(7) 13 + 2 =

(8) 15 + 2 =

(9) 17 + 2 =

(10) 20 + 2 =

(11) 22 + 2 =

(12) 24 + 2 =

(13) 26 + 2 =

(14) 28 + 2 =

Adding 2

1+2 to 4+2

To parents

In order to understand the concept of adding 2, it is important that your child master number recitation and the ability to add 1 first. If he or she is having difficulty, please return to the section on adding 1. Starting with this page, your child will gain solid calculation abilities by repeatedly practicing addition formulas that include the number 2.

■ Add the numbers below.

(1) 1 + 2 =

(2) 2 + 2 =

(3) 3 + 2 =

(4) 4 + 2 =

(5) 1 + 2 =

(6) 3 + 2 =

(7) 2 + 2 =

(8) 4 + 2 =

(9) 2 + 2 =

(10) 3 + 2 =

(11) 1 + 2 =

(12) 4 + 2 =

(13) 1 + 2 =

(14) 3 + 2 =

(15) 4 + 2 =

(16) 2 + 2 =

(17) 3 + 2 =

(18) 4 + 2 =

(19) 2 + 2 =

(20) 1 + 2 =

| 1 | 2 | 3 | 4 | 5 | 6 | 7 | 8 | 9 | 10 |

5+2 to 8+2

■ Add the numbers below.

(1) $5 + 2 =$

(2) $6 + 2 =$

(3) $7 + 2 =$

(4) $8 + 2 =$

(5) $5 + 2 =$

(6) $7 + 2 =$

(7) $6 + 2 =$

(8) $8 + 2 =$

(9) $6 + 2 =$

(10) $8 + 2 =$

(11) $7 + 2 =$

(12) $5 + 2 =$

(13) $8 + 2 =$

(14) $7 + 2 =$

(15) $5 + 2 =$

(16) $6 + 2 =$

(17) $5 + 2 =$

(18) $8 + 2 =$

(19) $6 + 2 =$

(20) $7 + 2 =$

| 1 | 2 | 3 | 4 | 5 | 6 | 7 | 8 | 9 | 10 |

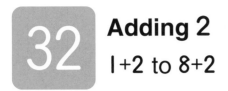

Adding 2
1+2 to 8+2

■ Add the numbers below.

(1) 1 + 2 =

(2) 3 + 2 =

(3) 4 + 2 =

(4) 2 + 2 =

(5) 6 + 2 =

(6) 5 + 2 =

(7) 7 + 2 =

(8) 8 + 2 =

(9) 4 + 2 =

(10) 5 + 2 =

(11) 7 + 2 =

(12) 6 + 2 =

(13) 8 + 2 =

(14) 2 + 2 =

(15) 1 + 2 =

(16) 3 + 2 =

(17) 1 + 2 =

(18) 6 + 2 =

(19) 4 + 2 =

(20) 7 + 2 =

| 1 | 2 | 3 | 4 | 5 | 6 | 7 | 8 | 9 | 10 |

■ Add the numbers below.

(1) 8 + 2 =

(2) 5 + 2 =

(3) 3 + 2 =

(4) 4 + 2 =

(5) 1 + 2 =

(6) 7 + 2 =

(7) 2 + 2 =

(8) 6 + 2 =

(9) 3 + 2 =

(10) 6 + 2 =

(11) 8 + 2 =

(12) 5 + 2 =

(13) 1 + 2 =

(14) 7 + 2 =

(15) 4 + 2 =

(16) 2 + 2 =

(17) 3 + 2 =

(18) 5 + 2 =

(19) 2 + 2 =

(20) 8 + 2 =

| 1 | 2 | 3 | 4 | 5 | 6 | 7 | 8 | 9 | 10 |

Adding 2
9+2 to 13+2

Name

Date

■ Add the numbers below.

(1) $9 + 2 =$

(2) $10 + 2 =$

(3) $11 + 2 =$

(4) $12 + 2 =$

(5) $13 + 2 =$

(6) $9 + 2 =$

(7) $11 + 2 =$

(8) $12 + 2 =$

(9) $10 + 2 =$

(10) $13 + 2 =$

(11) $11 + 2 =$

(12) $10 + 2 =$

(13) $9 + 2 =$

(14) $13 + 2 =$

(15) $12 + 2 =$

(16) $9 + 2 =$

(17) $13 + 2 =$

(18) $12 + 2 =$

(19) $10 + 2 =$

(20) $11 + 2 =$

| 11 | 12 | 13 | 14 | 15 |

14+2 to 18+2

■ Add the numbers below.

(1) $14 + 2 =$

(2) $15 + 2 =$

(3) $16 + 2 =$

(4) $17 + 2 =$

(5) $18 + 2 =$

(6) $15 + 2 =$

(7) $14 + 2 =$

(8) $17 + 2 =$

(9) $16 + 2 =$

(10) $18 + 2 =$

(11) $16 + 2 =$

(12) $17 + 2 =$

(13) $15 + 2 =$

(14) $18 + 2 =$

(15) $14 + 2 =$

(16) $17 + 2 =$

(17) $15 + 2 =$

(18) $18 + 2 =$

(19) $16 + 2 =$

(20) $14 + 2 =$

| 11 | 12 | 13 | 14 | 15 | 16 | 17 | 18 | 19 | 20 |

Adding 2

9+2 to *18+2*

Name

Date

■ Add the numbers below.

(1) 9 + 2 =

(2) 10 + 2 =

(3) 11 + 2 =

(4) 12 + 2 =

(5) 14 + 2 =

(6) 13 + 2 =

(7) 16 + 2 =

(8) 17 + 2 =

(9) 15 + 2 =

(10) 18 + 2 =

(11) 15 + 2 =

(12) 17 + 2 =

(13) 9 + 2 =

(14) 11 + 2 =

(15) 13 + 2 =

(16) 12 + 2 =

(17) 14 + 2 =

(18) 16 + 2 =

(19) 18 + 2 =

(20) 10 + 2 =

| 11 | 12 | 13 | 14 | 15 | 16 | 17 | 18 | 19 | 20 |

■ Add the numbers below.

(1) $15 + 2 =$

(2) $13 + 2 =$

(3) $17 + 2 =$

(4) $16 + 2 =$

(5) $10 + 2 =$

(6) $9 + 2 =$

(7) $14 + 2 =$

(8) $12 + 2 =$

(9) $18 + 2 =$

(10) $11 + 2 =$

(11) $9 + 2 =$

(12) $16 + 2 =$

(13) $12 + 2 =$

(14) $14 + 2 =$

(15) $18 + 2 =$

(16) $11 + 2 =$

(17) $13 + 2 =$

(18) $10 + 2 =$

(19) $17 + 2 =$

(20) $15 + 2 =$

| 11 | 12 | 13 | 14 | 15 | 16 | 17 | 18 | 19 | 20 |

35 Adding 2
1+2 to 18+2

Name

Date

■ Add the numbers below.

(1) 5 + 2 =

(2) 3 + 2 =

(3) 7 + 2 =

(4) 1 + 2 =

(5) 4 + 2 =

(6) 2 + 2 =

(7) 8 + 2 =

(8) 6 + 2 =

(9) 11 + 2 =

(10) 13 + 2 =

(11) 9 + 2 =

(12) 12 + 2 =

(13) 14 + 2 =

(14) 10 + 2 =

(15) 17 + 2 =

(16) 18 + 2 =

(17) 15 + 2 =

(18) 16 + 2 =

(19) 5 + 2 =

(20) 8 + 2 =

| 1 | 2 | 3 | 4 | 5 | 6 | 7 | 8 | 9 | 10 | 11 | 12 | 13 | 14 | 15 | 16 | 17 | 18 | 19 | 20 |

■ Add the numbers below.

(1) $11 + 2 =$

(2) $8 + 2 =$

(3) $16 + 2 =$

(4) $12 + 2 =$

(5) $7 + 2 =$

(6) $10 + 2 =$

(7) $4 + 2 =$

(8) $13 + 2 =$

(9) $3 + 2 =$

(10) $18 + 2 =$

(11) $9 + 2 =$

(12) $14 + 2 =$

(13) $5 + 2 =$

(14) $17 + 2 =$

(15) $1 + 2 =$

(16) $15 + 2 =$

(17) $2 + 2 =$

(18) $6 + 2 =$

(19) $4 + 2 =$

(20) $9 + 2 =$

| 1 | 2 | 3 | 4 | 5 | 6 | 7 | 8 | 9 | 10 | 11 | 12 | 13 | 14 | 15 | 16 | 17 | 18 | 19 | 20 |

1+2 to 18+2

36 Adding 2
19+2 to 23+2

Name

Date

■ Add the numbers below.

(1) $19 + 2 =$

(2) $20 + 2 =$

(3) $21 + 2 =$

(4) $22 + 2 =$

(5) $23 + 2 =$

(6) $21 + 2 =$

(7) $19 + 2 =$

(8) $20 + 2 =$

(9) $22 + 2 =$

(10) $23 + 2 =$

(11) $21 + 2 =$

(12) $20 + 2 =$

(13) $19 + 2 =$

(14) $23 + 2 =$

(15) $22 + 2 =$

(16) $20 + 2 =$

(17) $23 + 2 =$

(18) $19 + 2 =$

(19) $22 + 2 =$

(20) $21 + 2 =$

24+2 to 28+2

■ Add the numbers below.

(1) $24 + 2 =$

(2) $25 + 2 =$

(3) $26 + 2 =$

(4) $27 + 2 =$

(5) $28 + 2 =$

(6) $25 + 2 =$

(7) $24 + 2 =$

(8) $26 + 2 =$

(9) $27 + 2 =$

(10) $28 + 2 =$

(11) $26 + 2 =$

(12) $27 + 2 =$

(13) $25 + 2 =$

(14) $24 + 2 =$

(15) $28 + 2 =$

(16) $27 + 2 =$

(17) $25 + 2 =$

(18) $28 + 2 =$

(19) $26 + 2 =$

(20) $24 + 2 =$

| 21 | 22 | 23 | 24 | 25 | 26 | 27 | 28 | 29 | 30 |

37 Adding 2
19+2 to 28+2

Name

Date

■ Add the numbers below.

(1) 19 + 2 =

(2) 22 + 2 =

(3) 20 + 2 =

(4) 21 + 2 =

(5) 24 + 2 =

(6) 23 + 2 =

(7) 27 + 2 =

(8) 25 + 2 =

(9) 26 + 2 =

(10) 28 + 2 =

(11) 24 + 2 =

(12) 23 + 2 =

(13) 22 + 2 =

(14) 27 + 2 =

(15) 21 + 2 =

(16) 25 + 2 =

(17) 28 + 2 =

(18) 20 + 2 =

(19) 19 + 2 =

(20) 26 + 2 =

21 22 23 24 25 26 27 28 29 30

■ Add the numbers below.

(1) $20 + 2 =$

(2) $24 + 2 =$

(3) $28 + 2 =$

(4) $22 + 2 =$

(5) $25 + 2 =$

(6) $27 + 2 =$

(7) $21 + 2 =$

(8) $26 + 2 =$

(9) $23 + 2 =$

(10) $19 + 2 =$

(11) $28 + 2 =$

(12) $24 + 2 =$

(13) $19 + 2 =$

(14) $27 + 2 =$

(15) $23 + 2 =$

(16) $21 + 2 =$

(17) $26 + 2 =$

(18) $22 + 2 =$

(19) $20 + 2 =$

(20) $25 + 2 =$

21 22 23 24 25 26 27 28 29 30

Adding 2

9+2 to 28+2

Name	
Date	

■ Add the numbers below.

(1) 19 + 2 =

(2) 12 + 2 =

(3) 21 + 2 =

(4) 25 + 2 =

(5) 9 + 2 =

(6) 28 + 2 =

(7) 15 + 2 =

(8) 22 + 2 =

(9) 10 + 2 =

(10) 20 + 2 =

(11) 17 + 2 =

(12) 26 + 2 =

(13) 11 + 2 =

(14) 23 + 2 =

(15) 13 + 2 =

(16) 18 + 2 =

(17) 16 + 2 =

(18) 24 + 2 =

(19) 14 + 2 =

(20) 27 + 2 =

| 11 | 12 | 13 | 14 | 15 | 16 | 17 | 18 | 19 | 20 | 21 | 22 | 23 | 24 | 25 | 26 | 27 | 28 | 29 | 30 |

■ Add the numbers below.

(1) 25 + 2 =

(2) 15 + 2 =

(3) 27 + 2 =

(4) 23 + 2 =

(5) 9 + 2 =

(6) 13 + 2 =

(7) 18 + 2 =

(8) 24 + 2 =

(9) 11 + 2 =

(10) 12 + 2 =

(11) 21 + 2 =

(12) 19 + 2 =

(13) 10 + 2 =

(14) 14 + 2 =

(15) 26 + 2 =

(16) 17 + 2 =

(17) 22 + 2 =

(18) 20 + 2 =

(19) 16 + 2 =

(20) 28 + 2 =

| 11 | 12 | 13 | 14 | 15 | 16 | 17 | 18 | 19 | 20 | 21 | 22 | 23 | 24 | 25 | 26 | 27 | 28 | 29 | 30 |

Review
Adding 1 and 2

Name

Date

To parents
Starting with this page, your child will review addition with the numbers 1 and 2. If he or she is having difficulty, please return to previous pages for further practice. If your child encounters no difficulty solving these problems, it means he or she thoroughly understands the concept of adding 1 and 2 to other numbers. Please offer lots of praise.

■ Add the numbers below.

(1) $1 + 1 =$

(2) $6 + 1 =$

(3) $10 + 1 =$

(4) $13 + 1 =$

(5) $17 + 1 =$

(6) $20 + 1 =$

(7) $23 + 1 =$

(8) $24 + 1 =$

(9) $27 + 1 =$

(10) $28 + 1 =$

(11) $2 + 2 =$

(12) $7 + 2 =$

(13) $10 + 2 =$

(14) $14 + 2 =$

(15) $18 + 2 =$

(16) $20 + 2 =$

(17) $21 + 2 =$

(18) $23 + 2 =$

(19) $26 + 2 =$

(20) $28 + 2 =$

Add the numbers below.

(1) $2 + 1 =$

(2) $5 + 1 =$

(3) $7 + 1 =$

(4) $14 + 1 =$

(5) $18 + 1 =$

(6) $3 + 2 =$

(7) $6 + 2 =$

(8) $12 + 2 =$

(9) $15 + 2 =$

(10) $17 + 2 =$

(11) $21 + 1 =$

(12) $22 + 1 =$

(13) $25 + 1 =$

(14) $26 + 1 =$

(15) $29 + 1 =$

(16) $19 + 2 =$

(17) $22 + 2 =$

(18) $24 + 2 =$

(19) $25 + 2 =$

(20) $27 + 2 =$

40 Review

Adding 1 and 2

Name

Date

■ Add the numbers below.

(1) $3 + 1 =$

(2) $1 + 2 =$

(3) $7 + 1 =$

(4) $3 + 2 =$

(5) $7 + 2 =$

(6) $9 + 1 =$

(7) $11 + 2 =$

(8) $11 + 1 =$

(9) $16 + 2 =$

(10) $20 + 2 =$

(11) $19 + 1 =$

(12) $22 + 1 =$

(13) $22 + 2 =$

(14) $24 + 1 =$

(15) $25 + 1 =$

(16) $23 + 2 =$

(17) $27 + 1 =$

(18) $26 + 2 =$

(19) $28 + 1 =$

(20) $27 + 2 =$

■ Add the numbers below.

(1) $2 + 1 =$

(2) $2 + 2 =$

(3) $4 + 1 =$

(4) $6 + 2 =$

(5) $8 + 1 =$

(6) $12 + 1 =$

(7) $8 + 2 =$

(8) $13 + 2 =$

(9) $16 + 1 =$

(10) $18 + 2 =$

(11) $20 + 1 =$

(12) $19 + 2 =$

(13) $21 + 1 =$

(14) $23 + 1 =$

(15) $21 + 2 =$

(16) $26 + 1 =$

(17) $24 + 2 =$

(18) $29 + 1 =$

(19) $25 + 2 =$

(20) $28 + 2 =$

KUM☺N

Certificate of Achievement

is hereby congratulated on completing

My Book of Simple Addition

Presented on _____, 20____

_____
Parent or Guardian

3 + 2 = 5